THIS APOINTMENT LOGBOOK
BELONGS TO:

NAME:
_____

ADDRESS:
_____

_____

_____

CLIENT APPOINTMENT LOG

DATE	TIME	CLIENT NAME	PHONE	SERVICE	PRICE

CLIENT APPOINTMENT LOG

DATE	TIME	CLENT NAME	PHONE	SERVICE	PRICE

CLIENT APPOINTMENT LOG

DATE	TIME	CLENT NAME	PHONE	SERVICE	PRICE

CLIENT APPOINTMENT LOG

DATE	TIME	CLENT NAME	PHONE	SERVICE	PRICE

CLIENT APPOINTMENT LOG

DATE	TIME	CLENT NAME	PHONE	SERVICE	PRICE

CLIENT APPOINTMENT LOG

DATE	TIME	CLENT NAME	PHONE	SERVICE	PRICE

CLIENT APPOINTMENT LOG

DATE	TIME	CLENT NAME	PHONE	SERVICE	PRICE

CLIENT APPOINTMENT LOG

DATE	TIME	CLENT NAME	PHONE	SERVICE	PRICE

CLIENT APPOINTMENT LOG

DATE	TIME	CLENT NAME	PHONE	SERVICE	PRICE

CLIENT APPOINTMENT LOG

DATE	TIME	CLENT NAME	PHONE	SERVICE	PRICE

CLIENT APPOINTMENT LOG

DATE	TIME	CLENT NAME	PHONE	SERVICE	PRICE

CLIENT APPOINTMENT LOG

DATE	TIME	CLENT NAME	PHONE	SERVICE	PRICE

CLIENT APPOINTMENT LOG

DATE	TIME	CLIENT NAME	PHONE	SERVICE	PRICE

CLIENT APPOINTMENT LOG

DATE	TIME	CLENT NAME	PHONE	SERVICE	PRICE

CLIENT APPOINTMENT LOG

DATE	TIME	CLENT NAME	PHONE	SERVICE	PRICE

CLIENT APPOINTMENT LOG

DATE	TIME	CLIENT NAME	PHONE	SERVICE	PRICE

CLIENT APPOINTMENT LOG

DATE	TIME	CLENT NAME	PHONE	SERVICE	PRICE

CLIENT APPOINTMENT LOG

DATE	TIME	CLENT NAME	PHONE	SERVICE	PRICE

CLIENT APPOINTMENT LOG

DATE	TIME	CLENT NAME	PHONE	SERVICE	PRICE

CLIENT APPOINTMENT LOG

DATE	TIME	CLENT NAME	PHONE	SERVICE	PRICE

CLIENT APPOINTMENT LOG

DATE	TIME	CLENT NAME	PHONE	SERVICE	PRICE

CLIENT APPOINTMENT LOG

DATE	TIME	CLENT NAME	PHONE	SERVICE	PRICE

CLIENT APPOINTMENT LOG

DATE	TIME	CLENT NAME	PHONE	SERVICE	PRICE

CLIENT APPOINTMENT LOG

DATE	TIME	CLENT NAME	PHONE	SERVICE	PRICE

CLIENT APPOINTMENT LOG

DATE	TIME	CLENT NAME	PHONE	SERVICE	PRICE

CLIENT APPOINTMENT LOG

DATE	TIME	CLENT NAME	PHONE	SERVICE	PRICE

CLIENT APPOINTMENT LOG

DATE	TIME	CLENT NAME	PHONE	SERVICE	PRICE

CLIENT APPOINTMENT LOG

DATE	TIME	CLENT NAME	PHONE	SERVICE	PRICE

CLIENT APPOINTMENT LOG

DATE	TIME	CLENT NAME	PHONE	SERVICE	PRICE

CLIENT APPOINTMENT LOG

DATE	TIME	CLENT NAME	PHONE	SERVICE	PRICE

CLIENT APPOINTMENT LOG

DATE	TIME	CLENT NAME	PHONE	SERVICE	PRICE

CLIENT APPOINTMENT LOG

DATE	TIME	CLENT NAME	PHONE	SERVICE	PRICE

CLIENT APPOINTMENT LOG

DATE	TIME	CLENT NAME	PHONE	SERVICE	PRICE

CLIENT APPOINTMENT LOG

DATE	TIME	CLENT NAME	PHONE	SERVICE	PRICE

CLIENT APPOINTMENT LOG

DATE	TIME	CLENT NAME	PHONE	SERVICE	PRICE

CLIENT APPOINTMENT LOG

DATE	TIME	CLENT NAME	PHONE	SERVICE	PRICE

CLIENT APPOINTMENT LOG

DATE	TIME	CLENT NAME	PHONE	SERVICE	PRICE

CLIENT APPOINTMENT LOG

DATE	TIME	CLENT NAME	PHONE	SERVICE	PRICE

CLIENT APPOINTMENT LOG

DATE	TIME	CLENT NAME	PHONE	SERVICE	PRICE

CLIENT APPOINTMENT LOG

DATE	TIME	CLENT NAME	PHONE	SERVICE	PRICE

CLIENT APPOINTMENT LOG

DATE	TIME	CLENT NAME	PHONE	SERVICE	PRICE

CLIENT APPOINTMENT LOG

DATE	TIME	CLENT NAME	PHONE	SERVICE	PRICE

CLIENT APPOINTMENT LOG

DATE	TIME	CLENT NAME	PHONE	SERVICE	PRICE

CLIENT APPOINTMENT LOG

DATE	TIME	CLENT NAME	PHONE	SERVICE	PRICE

CLIENT APPOINTMENT LOG

DATE	TIME	CLENT NAME	PHONE	SERVICE	PRICE

CLIENT APPOINTMENT LOG

DATE	TIME	CLENT NAME	PHONE	SERVICE	PRICE

CLIENT APPOINTMENT LOG

DATE	TIME	CLENT NAME	PHONE	SERVICE	PRICE

CLIENT APPOINTMENT LOG

DATE	TIME	CLENT NAME	PHONE	SERVICE	PRICE

CLIENT APPOINTMENT LOG

DATE	TIME	CLIENT NAME	PHONE	SERVICE	PRICE

CLIENT APPOINTMENT LOG

DATE	TIME	CLENT NAME	PHONE	SERVICE	PRICE

CLIENT APPOINTMENT LOG

DATE	TIME	CLENT NAME	PHONE	SERVICE	PRICE

CLIENT APPOINTMENT LOG

DATE	TIME	CLENT NAME	PHONE	SERVICE	PRICE

CLIENT APPOINTMENT LOG

DATE	TIME	CLENT NAME	PHONE	SERVICE	PRICE

CLIENT APPOINTMENT LOG

DATE	TIME	CLENT NAME	PHONE	SERVICE	PRICE

CLIENT APPOINTMENT LOG

DATE	TIME	CLENT NAME	PHONE	SERVICE	PRICE

CLIENT APPOINTMENT LOG

DATE	TIME	CLENT NAME	PHONE	SERVICE	PRICE

CLIENT APPOINTMENT LOG

DATE	TIME	CLENT NAME	PHONE	SERVICE	PRICE

CLIENT APPOINTMENT LOG

DATE	TIME	CLENT NAME	PHONE	SERVICE	PRICE

CLIENT APPOINTMENT LOG

DATE	TIME	CLENT NAME	PHONE	SERVICE	PRICE

CLIENT APPOINTMENT LOG

DATE	TIME	CLENT NAME	PHONE	SERVICE	PRICE

CLIENT APPOINTMENT LOG

DATE	TIME	CLENT NAME	PHONE	SERVICE	PRICE

CLIENT APPOINTMENT LOG

DATE	TIME	CLENT NAME	PHONE	SERVICE	PRICE

CLIENT APPOINTMENT LOG

DATE	TIME	CLENT NAME	PHONE	SERVICE	PRICE

CLIENT APPOINTMENT LOG

DATE	TIME	CLENT NAME	PHONE	SERVICE	PRICE

CLIENT APPOINTMENT LOG

DATE	TIME	CLENT NAME	PHONE	SERVICE	PRICE

CLIENT APPOINTMENT LOG

DATE	TIME	CLENT NAME	PHONE	SERVICE	PRICE

CLIENT APPOINTMENT LOG

DATE	TIME	CLENT NAME	PHONE	SERVICE	PRICE

CLIENT APPOINTMENT LOG

DATE	TIME	CLENT NAME	PHONE	SERVICE	PRICE

CLIENT APPOINTMENT LOG

DATE	TIME	CLENT NAME	PHONE	SERVICE	PRICE

CLIENT APPOINTMENT LOG

DATE	TIME	CLENT NAME	PHONE	SERVICE	PRICE

CLIENT APPOINTMENT LOG

DATE	TIME	CLENT NAME	PHONE	SERVICE	PRICE

CLIENT APPOINTMENT LOG

DATE	TIME	CLENT NAME	PHONE	SERVICE	PRICE

CLIENT APPOINTMENT LOG

DATE	TIME	CLENT NAME	PHONE	SERVICE	PRICE

CLIENT APPOINTMENT LOG

DATE	TIME	CLENT NAME	PHONE	SERVICE	PRICE

CLIENT APPOINTMENT LOG

DATE	TIME	CLENT NAME	PHONE	SERVICE	PRICE

CLIENT APPOINTMENT LOG

DATE	TIME	CLIENT NAME	PHONE	SERVICE	PRICE

CLIENT APPOINTMENT LOG

DATE	TIME	CLENT NAME	PHONE	SERVICE	PRICE

CLIENT APPOINTMENT LOG

DATE	TIME	CLENT NAME	PHONE	SERVICE	PRICE

CLIENT APPOINTMENT LOG

DATE	TIME	CLENT NAME	PHONE	SERVICE	PRICE

CLIENT APPOINTMENT LOG

DATE	TIME	CLENT NAME	PHONE	SERVICE	PRICE

CLIENT APPOINTMENT LOG

DATE	TIME	CLENT NAME	PHONE	SERVICE	PRICE

CLIENT APPOINTMENT LOG

DATE	TIME	CLENT NAME	PHONE	SERVICE	PRICE

CLIENT APPOINTMENT LOG

DATE	TIME	CLENT NAME	PHONE	SERVICE	PRICE

CLIENT APPOINTMENT LOG

DATE	TIME	CLENT NAME	PHONE	SERVICE	PRICE

CLIENT APPOINTMENT LOG

DATE	TIME	CLENT NAME	PHONE	SERVICE	PRICE

CLIENT APPOINTMENT LOG

DATE	TIME	CLENT NAME	PHONE	SERVICE	PRICE

CLIENT APPOINTMENT LOG

DATE	TIME	CLENT NAME	PHONE	SERVICE	PRICE

CLIENT APPOINTMENT LOG

DATE	TIME	CLENT NAME	PHONE	SERVICE	PRICE

CLIENT APPOINTMENT LOG

DATE	TIME	CLENT NAME	PHONE	SERVICE	PRICE

CLIENT APPOINTMENT LOG

DATE	TIME	CLENT NAME	PHONE	SERVICE	PRICE

CLIENT APPOINTMENT LOG

DATE	TIME	CLENT NAME	PHONE	SERVICE	PRICE

CLIENT APPOINTMENT LOG

DATE	TIME	CLENT NAME	PHONE	SERVICE	PRICE

CLIENT APPOINTMENT LOG

DATE	TIME	CLENT NAME	PHONE	SERVICE	PRICE

CLIENT APPOINTMENT LOG

DATE	TIME	CLENT NAME	PHONE	SERVICE	PRICE

CLIENT APPOINTMENT LOG

DATE	TIME	CLENT NAME	PHONE	SERVICE	PRICE

CLIENT APPOINTMENT LOG

DATE	TIME	CLENT NAME	PHONE	SERVICE	PRICE

CLIENT APPOINTMENT LOG

DATE	TIME	CLENT NAME	PHONE	SERVICE	PRICE

CLIENT APPOINTMENT LOG

DATE	TIME	CLENT NAME	PHONE	SERVICE	PRICE

CLIENT APPOINTMENT LOG

DATE	TIME	CLENT NAME	PHONE	SERVICE	PRICE

CLIENT APPOINTMENT LOG

DATE	TIME	CLENT NAME	PHONE	SERVICE	PRICE

CLIENT APPOINTMENT LOG

DATE	TIME	CLENT NAME	PHONE	SERVICE	PRICE

CLIENT APPOINTMENT LOG

DATE	TIME	CLENT NAME	PHONE	SERVICE	PRICE

CLIENT APPOINTMENT LOG

DATE	TIME	CLENT NAME	PHONE	SERVICE	PRICE

CLIENT APPOINTMENT LOG

DATE	TIME	CLENT NAME	PHONE	SERVICE	PRICE

CLIENT APPOINTMENT LOG

DATE	TIME	CLENT NAME	PHONE	SERVICE	PRICE

CLIENT APPOINTMENT LOG

DATE	TIME	CLENT NAME	PHONE	SERVICE	PRICE

CLIENT APPOINTMENT LOG

DATE	TIME	CLENT NAME	PHONE	SERVICE	PRICE

CLIENT APPOINTMENT LOG

DATE	TIME	CLENT NAME	PHONE	SERVICE	PRICE

CLIENT APPOINTMENT LOG

DATE	TIME	CLENT NAME	PHONE	SERVICE	PRICE

CLIENT APPOINTMENT LOG

DATE	TIME	CLENT NAME	PHONE	SERVICE	PRICE

CLIENT APPOINTMENT LOG

DATE	TIME	CLENT NAME	PHONE	SERVICE	PRICE

CLIENT APPOINTMENT LOG

DATE	TIME	CLENT NAME	PHONE	SERVICE	PRICE

CLIENT APPOINTMENT LOG

DATE	TIME	CLENT NAME	PHONE	SERVICE	PRICE

CLIENT APPOINTMENT LOG

DATE	TIME	CLENT NAME	PHONE	SERVICE	PRICE

CLIENT APPOINTMENT LOG

DATE	TIME	CLENT NAME	PHONE	SERVICE	PRICE

CLIENT APPOINTMENT LOG

DATE	TIME	CLIENT NAME	PHONE	SERVICE	PRICE

CLIENT APPOINTMENT LOG

DATE	TIME	CLENT NAME	PHONE	SERVICE	PRICE

CLIENT APPOINTMENT LOG

DATE	TIME	CLENT NAME	PHONE	SERVICE	PRICE

CLIENT APPOINTMENT LOG

DATE	TIME	CLENT NAME	PHONE	SERVICE	PRICE